MY RAINCOAT HAS A SILVER LINING

WRITTEN BY STEPHANIE REITZ

ILLUSTRATED BY TOBY MIKLE

For Mom, Dad, Carolyn
and my husband Bill
-- with love and gratitude

Celia

Celia likes to run in circles
it's her favorite thing to do
big circles, little ones
wearing her red patent leather shoes.

Celia likes to run in circles
she just keeps goin' round
she doesn't seem to look at much
except the pattern she makes on the ground.

Celia likes to run in circles
giggling with glee
her friends watch and ask themselves
what could be so funny?

Celia likes to run in circles
it keeps her very busy
but if those circles get too small
it makes her very dizzy.

Celia likes to run in circles
it's her favorite thing to do
and if you're not very careful
she'll run circles around you!

Boogie Boarding

Do you know what to do with a boogie board?
Do you dance with it, prance with it, or even take a chance with it?
Do you tease it, squeeze it, or perhaps rake the leaves with it?

What do you do with a boogie board?
Do you throw it, show it, or shovel mounds of snow with it?
Do you fold it, hold it, or search for hidden gold with it?

I don't know how to use a boogie board
and I'm afraid it shows
because no matter how I try
I can't get it up my nose.

Which is the Way?

Which is the way
to the Island of Fey?
I can't find it here on the map.

I've searched high and low
for that isle I love so
with this atlas spread on my lap.

There the Gigahees dance
and the Yabahoos prance
and I join as the Bakadoos clap.

I can hardly wait
'cause I stay up so late
and eat marshmallows out of my cap.

I chase pointy stars
and drive one-wheeled cars
once you learn how it's a snap!

Oh wait, now I know
there's just one way to go
Mom, is it time for my nap?

Knock-Knock Jokes

I like knock-knock jokes
Do you like knock-knock jokes?
I think they're lots of fun.

I like roller skates
Do you like roller skates?
I skate faster than I run.

I like hot dogs
Do you like hot dogs?
I eat them on a bun.

I like knock-knock jokes
Do you like knock-knock jokes?
Well this poem isn't one.

Dress Up

Stripes and polka dots
Stripes and polka dots
I get so tired of stripes and polka dots.

How about green
with a splash of blue?
Or even plain white
with some lilac will do.

I really like orange
but it can be bright
what if I promise
to wear it only at night?

I know, I've got it
I can wear pink
see, it matches my cheeks
what do you think?

Please can we come to some agreement
I'm not asking for a lot
but I'm tired of always wearing
stripes and polka dots.

Talent Show

Step - together - step - together - step - together - CLAP!
Sis says I can learn to dance if I practice that.

Step - together - step - together - step - together - KICK!
Sis says not to let my leg hit the floor like a brick.

Step - together - step - together - step - together - TWIRL!
I think I'm an excellent brother for giving this a whirl.

Step - together - step - together - step - together - SLIDE!
Sis says when I do that, I should stretch my legs real wide.

Step - together - step - together - step - together - WHOA!
No way am I performing in her backyard talent show!

My Raincoat Has a Silver Lining

The weather may not be hot
and I know that it rains a lot
but in my head the sun is shining
because my raincoat has a silver lining.

I cuff the sleeves so my friends can see
the silver shining so prettily
the outside is red like a ruby jewel
it's my favorite thing to wear to school.

It has buttons on the front and a hood on the back
it's easy to spot it on the coat rack
it's warm and cozy and fun to wear
I clean it and fold it and take great care.

The pockets are big and go very deep
a good place for things I want to keep
like my tissue and my lollipop
and my pencil with the blue eraser top.

I don't want to outgrow it anytime soon
please let it fit at least until June
otherwise I will start to pout
hey, maybe I can stretch it out.

I know I can't wear the coat forever
even in the stormy weather
but that's okay, I'll still be smiling
because my raincoat has a silver lining.

Teacher

My teacher says I'm very smart
and I know it's true
'cause I can say my alphabet
and know one plus one is two.

My teacher says I'm very strong
and I know she's right
'cause I can climb the jungle gym
using all my might.

My teacher says I'm very fast
and I know that's a fact
'cause when we run around the yard
I'm always the first one back.

My teacher tells me such nice things
maybe I'm a goddess
but my teacher also tells me
I should learn to be more modest.

Away We Go

I know how to drive
just watch me go
I steer my go-cart in the snow.

Whisshhh, whoosh, whee, wow
I'm really going fast now.

I ran over the lanes
that I set up with sticks
but that's okay
they're easy to fix.

Whisshhh, whoosh, whee, wow
I'm really going fast now.

The snow is blowing in my face
my nose is getting red
I wonder if all drivers
wear wool caps on their heads.

Whisshhh, whoosh, whee, wow
I'm really going fast now.

I've gone so far down this hill
I can no longer see my street
it's an uphill climb back to the house
glad I have warm boots on my feet.

I start to climb
how much farther to go?
I sure hope Mom makes me a hot cocoa.

Yellow

I met a fellow
whose name is yellow
a cheery sort
who laughs with a snort.

We play together after school
I swim with him at the pool
he keeps me company when I ride my bike
just the two of us traveling down the pike.

Things seem different when he's not around
there's a shadow on the ground
without him my days aren't as fun
I really love my friend the sun!

Spaceship

I'm going to build a spaceship
thought little Elsie Lou
so I can travel to the stars
like all the astronauts do.

I wonder what stars will look like
when I see them so nearby
are they pink and silver jewels
hanging in the sky?

How would it feel if I reached out to touch?
Would they be hot or cold?
Maybe they're like tiny sparklers
on a shiny stick I can hold.

I know there are a lot of them
more than I can count
but that's okay, I have fun trying
to guess the right amount.

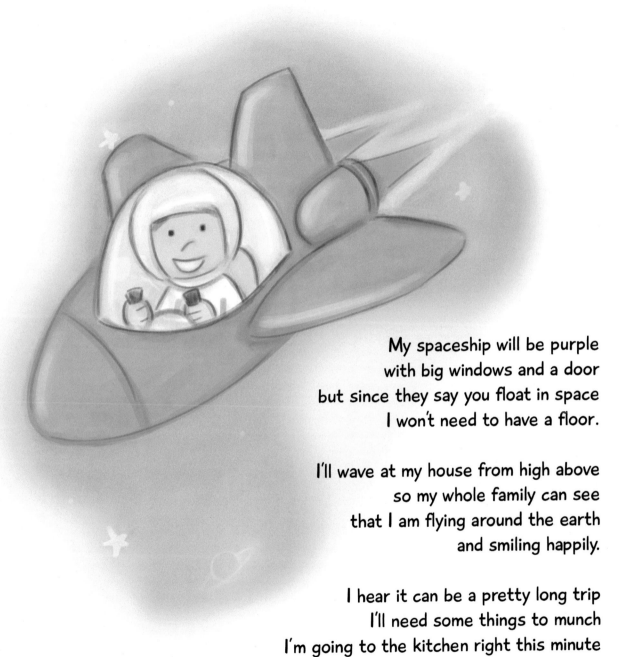

My spaceship will be purple
with big windows and a door
but since they say you float in space
I won't need to have a floor.

I'll wave at my house from high above
so my whole family can see
that I am flying around the earth
and smiling happily.

I hear it can be a pretty long trip
I'll need some things to munch
I'm going to the kitchen right this minute
and pack myself a lunch.

Stevie and the Sea

Stevie sits and looks at the sea
he wonders how many fish there could be
bouncing and rolling and riding on waves
and swimming through treasures in underground caves.

Stevie would like to swim along too
in the water so green and blue
if only he'd worn his swimsuit today
he would follow the fish, they know the way.

Imagine the many things to explore
as he paddled along the ocean floor
he might find a starfish or a smooth pink shell
oh the stories he would tell!

Stevie sits on the beach and plays with the sand
patting it down with his hand
oh how he'd love to be in motion
splashing and diving in the ocean.

Who needs a swimsuit anyway?
He wouldn't ruin his Saturday.
Stevie jumped in wearing all of his clothes
and laughed when the water went up his nose.

The Way I See It

I say yes
You say no
I say because
You say, so?

You say cherry
I say lime
You say grape
I say, not this time!

I say fast
You say slow
I say wait
You say, go!

I say square
You say round
Then a scuffle
On the ground

I am short
Which you don't deny
Maybe when I grow
We'll see eye to eye?

Ant Farm

The ant farm is a busy place
with lots of activity all day
and only when the work is done
do the ants find time to play.

The planter ants put the seeds in the soil
and wait for something to grow
radishes, beans, corn on the cob
all arranged in beautiful rows.

The guardian ants keep animals away
especially those troublesome rabbits
they can't be allowed to eat the crop
or it might become a habit.

The harvest ants pull the plants from the ground
the crops are now ready to eat
they'll be sent to the grocery store
lots of veggies to go with your meat.

And don't forget the carrier ant
he has the toughest job of all
loading everything on the truck
and not letting anything fall.

It all works quite well
but still, I don't see much hope
how will that little ant
carry such a big cantaloupe?

Why?

I don't know why the answer is no
Mom says because she said so.

I don't think her decision is fair
all my friends are going to be there
but Mom says she doesn't care.

I tried hard to change her mind
used every argument I could find
but she's not being very kind.

I pout, I cry
but no matter how I try
I keep getting the same reply.

I can't wait until I'm grown
so I can make decisions on my own.